Coffee Shop Inspirations

"*Coffee Shop Inspirations* illustrates so well the practical use of the Word of God. The author has full confidence in God's inerrant Word, filtering everything through Scripture as the believer's final authority. This book is clear, balanced and faithful to Scripture. I recommend it to you for your encouragement in your daily walk with the Lord in the light of His Word."
~Dr. Gary Coombs, *President: Southern California Seminary*

This book will be a blessing to anyone who reads it and applies the material. The author's writing is inspiring, helpful, and is truly a self-help book in every sense of the word.
~Dr. Paul Fisher, *Pastor, Professor and licensed therapist.*

"Jed not only offers sound and biblical advice, but he does it in a way that is both immensely practical and immediately applicable."
~James Fazio, *Dean of Biblical Studies: Southern California Seminary*

Praise for
Coffee Shop Inspirations

"Jed has done a masterful of taking the truth of Scripture and the research behind psychology to show practical ways to impact everyday life. The insights shared are not theory but proven techniques which have been applied to real life. Everyone would profit from reading this book."
~Russ Cox, *Senior Pastor of New Hope Community Church*

"This particular project of Jed's is not only enlightening; it is spiritually grounded... Thank you for the *Coffee Shop* experience."
~Jonathan Dean, *MA, IMF, PsyD-Student*

"As an Assistant Pastor and therapist, I have enjoyed reading this book. Jed had been able to use his God given talents to bring light for both Christians and Psychotherapists. This is truly a must read for all."
~Carlos E. Magallon, *M.A., Ephesians 4:5 Ministries*

"Jed makes applying key principles from the Bible and psychology practical and easy."
~Jessica Daly, *IMF*

Inspirations

SIMPLE STRATEGIES FOR BUILDING DYNAMIC
LEADERSHIP &
RELATIONSHIPS

Jed Jurchenko

www.CoffeeShopConversations.com

© 2014 by Jed Jurchenko.

Printed by CreateSpace,
An Amazon.com Company
Available from Amazon.com
and other online stor

Practical tools from the Bible and psychology for thriving in leadership, relationships and life!

Dedication

To my wife, Jenny and daughters Mackenzie, Brookline, and Addison; I am truly blessed to have you in my life. Thank you for joining me on this ongoing adventure of learning how to love, lead, and live well

Contents

Introduction

Welcome to *Coffee Shop Inspirations*, a book that provides life-changing leadership and relationship skills in a fun and casual format. But before diving in, let me first introduce myself. My name is Jed Jurchenko. I'm a husband, a father to three girls, a marriage and family therapist, and a college professor. I have over a decade of experience in supporting children, teens and families in overcoming obstacles and moving forward in pursuit of their goals.

I consider it a privilege to be able to sit alongside those who are hurting and stuck in their personal growth and support them in breaking though barriers, regaining momentum and making life work—and this is exactly what we will do in the pages ahead. In this book you will find effective strategies for expanding your circle of influence, promoting positive relationships, and increasing the joyful moments in your life.

This book is entitled *Coffee Shop Inspirations* for a number of reasons. First, as you may have guessed, I appreciate a good cup of coffee, and my goal is that, like fine coffee, reading this book will be an enjoyable experience. After all, everyone learns best when they are having fun along the way. Second, coffee shops have a relaxed atmosphere, and I prefer to write in a casual, conversational style, as if you and I were sitting down in a local coffee shop, sipping on a hot beverage as we explored time-tested truths for living well. Although this book contains profound insights from theology and psychology, the goal is to always keep things simple and applicable.

My final objective is that, as you read, you will be inspired to take action. Much can be accomplished with a good set of tools, but only if they are taken out of the box and put to good use. It is my sincere desire that, in the chapters ahead, you will gain valuable skills that you can put into practice right away, and then experience for yourself the dynamic growth that results.

As we begin our journey, I invite you to unwind and grab a cup of coffee, tea or other favorite drink as we plan and dream about exciting ways to live out the life-changing principles found in the Bible and in psychology.

Sincerely,

COFFEE SHOP CONVERSATIONS

Chapter 1

Tools for Living Well

Over the past three years, I've had the privilege of teaching Bible and psychology classes at a tiny seminary in Southern California. One question frequently asked by students in the courses I teach is how, and if, the Bible and psychology go together. Perhaps you have wondered the same thing yourself. Sometimes Christ's followers are apprehensive about turning to psychology for support, seeing it as worldly and weird, or fearing that using principles of psychology will demonstrate a lack of faith in God.

I'm happy to share with you that this is not the case. The Bible and psychology are a dynamic duo that, like Batman and Robin, coffee and chocolate, and the beach and a beautiful summer day, pair very well together. They are powerful allies that team up to provide effective tools for making life work. In the chapters ahead, we'll examine five specific strategies from these two significant areas that can be immediately put into practice to:

- Reduce conflict,
- Increase your number of wise choices,
- Help you press through obstacles,
- Amplify your happiness, and
- Give you the tools needed to live well.

But before diving in, let's first explore why the fields of theology and psychology work so well together.

Three Reasons the Bible and Psychology Work Well Together

1. The Bible and psychology have the highest regard for truth and are packed with wisdom.

If we are going to live, lead, and relate well then following advice that is wise and true is of the utmost importance. Like many of Christ's followers, I believe the Bible is not just "a book," but "the book" when it comes to truth. 2 Timothy 3:16 says, "Every scripture is inspired by God." In the original Greek the word "inspiration" is "*theopnuestos*," which would be more literally and directly translated as, "God-breathed." According to 2 Timothy, the Bible is as much the word of God as if God had personally spoken each and every word it contains out of His own mouth. Inspiration makes the Bible unique and elevates it above all other books. Scripture is the ultimate source of truth and contains some of the most valuable wisdom on the planet because it was given to us by the author of life Himself. For those who are truly passionate about developing in the areas of leadership and relationship, looking to the Bible is a must.

As we will see, psychology and Scripture,

share a similar passion for wisdom and truth. Dictionary.com describes psychology as "the science of human and animal behavior." The word science is used in this definition because Psychology relies heavily on the scientific process. Each year psychologists put in thousands of hours conducting experiments, testing hypotheses, and gathering data for the purpose of uncovering truths that enhance our ability to make wise decisions. Of course, scientists don't always get everything right and sometimes corrections are made along the way, but the important thing is that truth is held in the highest regard. Truth matters and this is an area in which the Bible and psychology readily agree.

2. God created psychology.

I've read a number of books that describe the Bible as spiritual wisdom and psychology as secular wisdom, but this just isn't the case. As you can tell by now, I truly believe the Bible to be unique. It contains the words of God Himself and is packed with information that we could not otherwise know about ourselves and the world around us if God had not provided us with this incredible gift.

Yet Scripture is not God's only way of

revealing Himself. John 1:1 says, "All things were created by him (Jesus), and apart from him not one thing was created that has been created." Like a skilled painter who bears his soul in his work of art, the universe is God's masterpiece, which provides a glimpse into the splendor of our Creator. Because God created everything, all of the sciences, including astronomy, geology, physics, and psychology function on principles designed by Him. Science too is part of God's handiwork.

There are two passages from the Bible that further expound upon this. Roman's 1:20 says, "For since the creation of the world his invisible attributes—his eternal power and divine nature—have been clearly seen, because they are understood through what has been made." And Psalm 19:1 proclaims, "The heavens declare the glory of God; the sky displays his handiwork."

Truly, God's character is revealed through His creation. Psychology carefully studies this God-designed-universe by means of the scientific process in order to uncover truths about how His creatures function best. When viewed in this light, psychology becomes nothing short of a profoundly spiritual act.

3. The Bible and psychology are all about relationships.

One day, Jesus was asked to name the greatest commandment. Instead of providing one answer, He gave two, which are summed up in the phrase, *love God and love people*. Jesus proclaimed that these two concise commands encompass the entire law and prophets. That's 613 Old Testament ordinances encapsulated in five short words. But why did Jesus answer with two commands instead of one? Likely, it's because it is impossible to follow the first commandment without obeying the second. Humanity is God's prize creation. The book of Genesis tells how God fashioned mankind in His own image, and it's impossible to fully love God without caring for the crowning glory of His creation. Honoring God is all about relationships and involves not only relating well to God, but also connecting benevolently with others.

Psychology understands the value of relationships and provides practical insights that build on the foundation of biblical teachings. The Bible defines love, commands love, and provides us with the ultimate example of love in the form of Jesus Christ laying down His life for us. Yet, with all that the Bible teaches about love, it is not exhaustive. Life is complex, and without additional study, our understanding of what it means to put love into action amidst the intricacies of life would be left incomplete.

Those who are married can attest to this. For example, while one spouse would think it romantic to enter the house to find a home-cooked meal, lit candles adorning the table, and a rose-petal path leading from the front door to the bedroom, another would walk into the same scenario and wonder, *who is going to clean up this mess?* Each of us is uniquely fashioned. We have individual tastes and personalities that heavily influence the way we perceive the world. Because of this, it takes wisdom and discernment to relate to those around us in ways that are meaningful to them.

Further adding to this complexity is our distinct physiology. Psychology refers to us as biopsychosocial beings, meaning that our genetics, plus the thoughts in our heads, and the people to whom we are closely connected, interrelate to have major bearings on the ways that we think, feel, and act. The downside of this complexity is that it provides an open door for things to go amiss which results in stretches where life becomes utterly messy. Some examples of this include times when we or someone close to us is:

- Struggling with mental illness,
- Addicted to a harmful substance or activity (such as drugs, alcohol, gambling, etc.),
- Parenting a strong-willed child, or
- Dealing with any relationship where ongoing conflict occurs.

When these, and other complications of a similar magnitude, surface profound wisdom is needed in order to love well. Successfully navigating life's difficulties requires that we continually expand our understanding of love. In the chapters ahead, we'll explore strategies from psychology that build upon key teachings of Scripture to provide support in leading and relating well during times when easy answers are not readily available.

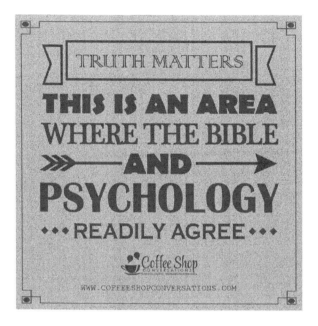

I hope that by now you're thoroughly convinced that, when it comes to leadership and relationships, the Bible and psychology each have much to offer. Now, let's look at five hands-on approaches for putting key principles from these two important areas into practice.

Chapter 2

Don't Pick up the Rope

Ever since I was a child, tug-o-war has been one of my favorite games. Growing up, our family had a rope that we kept in our garage especially for this purpose. The tug-o-war rope would make its appearance at birthday parties and special events a couple of times each year. In the game of tug-o-war, two teams holding on to opposite ends of the rope attempt to forcefully pull each other over a dividing line in the middle.

Our friends and family played these games with the utmost seriousness. After separating into two equal teams, each team member would firmly grasp their end of the rope with both hands, broaden their stance and resolutely fix their feet to the ground. The leader of the game would yell, "On your mark... get set... go!" And the tugging would begin.

One side would pull the other a few steps

forward. Then, the side that was pulled would find their balance and retaliate with a show of force that would cause the other side to lose ground. In a good game of tug-o-war, the two sides would heave each other back and forth a number of times before one side finally succeeded in dragging the other across the dividing-line, winning the game.

A good game of tug-o-war is a lot like a horrific argument. During quarrels, two sides tug and pull at each other an attempt to convince the other person to do something that he or she does not want to do. This tugging may come in the form of:

- Reasoning and logic
- Threats of consequences
- Bribes
- Yelling and outbursts of anger, and
- Passive-aggressive behaviors such as the silent treatment

The well-known psychologist and founder of choice theory, William Glasser, referred to these types of coercion as "external control psychology." The name is fitting because, through the implementation of these techniques, one person attempts to control the actions of another. Glasser theorized that the majority of problems that people face have relational issues at their core. The trouble with external control psychology is that it always damages the relationship, rarely gets us what we want, leads to the back-and-forth power struggles that resemble a really bad game of tug-o-war and, in the end, creates a situation where nobody walks away a winner.

If you've ever engaged in one of these messy back-and-forth arguments, you know that they are not a lot of fun and can be an enormous roadblock for relationships and accomplishments. However, if you observe the best leaders and relaters you will notice that these men and women have discovered how to dodge these energy-draining, time-consuming, tug-o-war arguments by putting into practice principles for disagreeing agreeably. Good leaders know how to hold on to their own opinions and keep much-needed boundaries intact with minimal conflict taking place. The good news is that anyone can learn these same skills and in many instances, the tools and techniques taught in this chapter will eliminate the games of verbal tug-o-war entirely. Imagine what it would be like to never enter into a back-and-forth disagreement again.

For some, this would mean hours spent

yelling, arguing, debating, bribing, punishing, begging, pleading, demanding and threatening could be used for more productive activities. Romans 12:18 says, "If possible, so far as it depends on you, live peaceably with all people." The skills taught in the next few pages will thoroughly equip you to put this verse into practice.

The benefit of the techniques you are about to learn is that they almost always work and the more you practice them, the better you will become. Practice is important because energy, creativity and intentionality are required in order to utilize these tools well. So what are these amazing strategies for preventing the outbreak of verbal tug-o-wars? The techniques are simple and all center on one key idea. Evading a malicious game of verbal tug-o-war is done by using the same skills involved in avoiding an actual game of tug-o-war—one simply doesn't pick up the rope.

I know this may sound too easy, but it works, and this tool is far from simplistic. Keeping our hands off the rope involves giving up the right to use external control psychology tactics and replacing these bad habits with new strategies for resolving disagreements.

Don't Pick Up the Rope!

Four Strategies for Avoiding the Rope

1. Offer choices.

No one likes to be told what to do, yet at times, rules and regulations must be enforced. Good parents impose healthy structures for their children to follow, including age-appropriate bedtimes, healthy eating habits and daily chores. Similarly, good leaders have the task of upholding the vision and mission of the company, which means that sometimes the word "no" can't be taken for an answer. During times when structure must be enforced and tensions rise, one way to avoid picking up the rope is to offer choices.

Being told exactly what to do and how to do it can trigger anxiety and cause the other person to feel powerless. On the other hand, offering options provides a sense of empowerment that can elevate the mood of the entire conversation. For example, instead of telling a three-year-old child, "It's time for bed," you might reinforce the rules of the home by providing two similar choices. One way to do this would be to state, "It's time for bed, would you like to walk to bed, or would you like Daddy to pick you up and fly you to bed?" If you try out this strategy, you may be surprised at how well it works. Likely you'll be figuring out a way to help your kiddo take flight as you gently guide him or her to bed, but this is a small price to pay for enforcing the structure in the home in a creative, fun and conflict-free manner.

2. Give empathy.

Showing empathy involves taking into account the feelings of others, walking a mile in their shoes, and asking ourselves how we would feel if we found ourselves facing similar circumstances. When we empathize with others, we are acknowledging their pain as real. Empathy is a powerful tool that supports others in feeling understood and lets them know we are on their side. The great thing about empathy is that we can provide it regardless of whether or not we agree with the other person's course of action because giving empathy is much different than offering agreement.

Imagine for a moment that a close friend goes against your sound advice and as a result of not heeding your words of wisdom, finds himself in the midst of an extraordinarily big mess. At this point, you could decide to point out the connection between your friend's choosing not follow your advice and the crisis that ensued by stating, "See, I told you so." But these words rarely produce positive results. A far better option would be to offer empathy. Although you may continue to emphatically disagree with the decisions that have been made, it's still quite possible to reach out with compassionate understanding by stating:

- I am so sorry you are going through this right now.
- This situation is really hard and I don't like what is happening to you.
- It makes me sad to see you hurting like this and I really wish things were different right now.
- I see that you are hurting and want you to know that I am here for you and on your side.

As you can see, empathy does not equal approval and there is nothing wrong with empathizing with someone's hurts when you disagree with their actions. A second reason people don't offer empathy is because they fear that if they empathize with the feelings of another, they are then obligated to become part of the solution. But this is not the case either. Offering compassionate understanding does not obligate us to fix the other person's problems. It's quite possible to provide empathy while still allowing someone to learn from his or her mistakes. Take for example, a dad who buys his teenage daughter an expensive cell phone. Then, a few days later, his daughter comes home in tears because she lost her phone.

Let's imagine that this dad avoids succumbing to the temptation to lecture, scold, shame and blame. Instead he offers empathy. Later, this daughter asks her dad to buy her a new cell-phone and Dad says "no." However, instead of accepting this answer, the daughter attempts to turn the conversation into a debate by bringing up all of the reasons why she absolutely needs a phone. This wise father sees the "rope" in plain sight. As much as he would like to offer a rebuttal to his daughter's arguments and begin a lecture on the importance of responsibility, he knows that this will only result in his daughter refining her tactics and offering up new arguments. So instead of engaging in this back-and-forth, tug-o-war he offers empathy over and over again by stating:

- I'm so sorry you lost your cell phone. Being without a phone is no fun, especially for a teenager.

- No, I can't buy you a new phone. You'll have to earn the money for a new one on your own. But I'm really sad that you don't have one.
- I know that it's really, really hard to be without a cell phone right now. I'd like to see you get a new phone really quickly too.
- I would be glad to brainstorm with you ideas to earn money to buy a new phone. Finding a job can be difficult, but I know you can do it and I want to be your biggest cheerleader.

What do you think would happen if a parent responded in this manner? At first, the child might try harder to engage in an argument, but if empathy is consistently offered, it will be almost impossible for a heated dispute to take place. It's extremely difficult to squabble with someone who continually acknowledges your pain, affirms their care for you and reinforces that they are on your side. Empathy is a valuable tool because it prevents a verbal tug-o-war from taking place while at the same time, strengthens the relationship.

3. Accentuate areas of agreement.

"You're right, ice cream does sound good right about now," I said. "Daddy, does that mean we can get one?" my six-year-old daughter enthusiastically asked for the second time. "No," I replied, "I already told you that we can't buy ice cream before lunch, but it sure does sound good. I'd get chocolate if I could, what flavor would you get?" These words began our lengthy conversation about our favorite flavors of ice-cream and how much we both like it, while at the same time, ended our debate about whether or not we could buy one.

If my daughter had continued to ask for ice cream that day, I would have persistently reinforced the structure of no ice cream before lunch, while also reiterating my love for this indulgence. Accentuating areas of agreement involves highlighting positives and commonalities without changing one's course of action. Every word I spoke on that hot summer day was 100 percent true. I really do love ice cream, chocolate is my favorite, and yes, ice cream before lunch certainly did sound delicious. However, on this particular occasion, I had chosen to reinforce the structure of healthy eating habits. As a result, the two of us agreed that ice cream sounded delicious. Then we enjoyed our lunch together and had a blast the rest of the day, without ever purchasing a single ice cream.

Accentuating areas of agreement validates the other person's ideas as important and steers the conversation away from a place of "you're wrong and I'm right," instead acknowledging that two people can have similar tastes and still come to different conclusions. Much like empathy, highlighting areas of agreement allows us to strengthen our bond with the other person without succumbing to their final conclusion. In most disagreements, similarities and dissimilarities exist. Tug-o-wars emphasize differences while this technique takes the opposite approach.

Those who use this tool are secure enough to know that it's possible to validate someone's ideas and still choose a different course of action. Accentuating areas of agreement is especially valuable because it gives us the freedom to disagree without becoming disagreeable in the process.

4. Allow teachable moments to take place.

I've lost count of the number of times I have witnessed parents get into long-standing battles with their teenage sons and daughters out of a desire to spare their children pain. The strategy of allowing teachable moments to take place is a powerful one. It is also a tool that should be used sparingly.

Leaders who allow teachable moments to take place choose their battles wisely. They understand that it's perfectly OK for others to be wrong. As a result, they provide those around them with the freedom to make and learn from their mistakes. For example, one mother of multiple teenagers I know assigns everyone in the household a chore and a weekly allowance. If a member of the household decides not to do their chore, they are free to pay someone else in the home to do it for them. Mom can occasionally be overheard saying, "If you don't want to do your chore, that's fine, and if no one else wants to do it, that's fine too. I'll gladly do your chore for you; just know that my fee will be higher than anyone else in the house." As far as I know, no one has ever taken Mom up on her offer. The chores always get done, sometimes by the person assigned the chore and sometimes by hiring out a sibling, but this doesn't happen often. Natural sibling rivalry is a powerful motivator. After all, it's pretty difficult to watch your siblings buy nice things with the money they earned from taking over your responsibility.

The use of this particular technique has resulted in disappointment for a few teenagers I know who found themselves without money for activities they wanted to do. On the other hand, it had the benefit of helping these same teens gain an understanding of the value of money and its connection to hard work and responsibility. Sometimes experience really is the best teacher. For strong-willed children, it might be better to allow them to try out a bad idea while they are still under your guidance so that you can help them pick up the pieces afterwards as opposed to having them wait until they move out of the home to put their flawed scheme into practice. Keep in mind, though, that this type of decision requires much prayer and thoughtful consideration before it is put into practice.

Ideally, children and adults learn from reason, logic and the past experiences of others. However, when this doesn't take place, it might be time to allow a teachable moment to happen. Those who use this technique understand that many differences of opinion are not worthy of an ongoing argument and choose their battles wisely. As a result, they sometimes make the intentional choice to give in, knowing that it is ok for others to be wrong and to learn from their mistakes.

Keeping Our Hands off the Rope

If you choose to use the techniques presented in this chapter, you'll quickly discover two things. First, I think you'll be pleasantly surprised to discover how well they work. When implemented with wisdom and tack, these four skills are an almost sure-fire way to avoid the verbal tug-o-war that external control psychology brings.

The second thing you'll notice is that keeping your hands off of the rope can be tricky. Conflict generates excitement and engagement. This is why every good reality television show is bursting at the seams with drama. The absence of conflict can seem boring at first, but avoid the temptation to give in. Couples who have made conflict their primary way of connecting with one another will soon realize they must put forth creativity and effort to learn new strategies for generating intimacy.

It can be difficult to resist the temptation to lecture, rationalize, demand, insist, plead, beg and cajole, especially during times when you are thoroughly convinced that you are right. The important thing to remember is that when techniques from external control psychology are used, even when you do succeed in getting your way, it will have come at the high cost of damaging the relationship. In verbal tug-o-wars, winning the battle often means losing the war. So next time you're tempted to tell someone they're wrong, think back to the strategies of offering choices, giving empathy, accentuating areas of agreement and allowing teachable moments to take place — and don't pick up the rope.

Chapter 3

Make the Best Bad Choice

Imagine for a moment that you and a group of coworkers are carpooling back to the office after attending a high-energy leadership seminar. The experience was energizing and you can't wait to implement all of the new tools and techniques you just learned. But as you embark on the lengthy return drive, you and your coworkers find yourselves stuck in rush-hour traffic. Before long, everyone in the car is hungry and the decision is made to stop for dinner.

Inching your way through the bumper to bumper sea of vehicles, you and your small band of weary travelers finally reach the next exit where, much to your dismay the only available stop for dinner happens to be the salt-laden, grease-covered restaurant chain *Fast Food is Us!* You think back to your New Year's resolution of losing ten pounds and how you have been so good about strictly adhering to the regulations of your diet up to this point. At first you're worried. Then you think to yourself, *Actually, this probably isn't too bad. 'Fast Food is Us' is delicious, and surely they will have a few healthy options on the menu.*

The only problem is they don't. As you look over the meal selections, you find yourself staring in wonder at a comprehensive inventory of deep-fried, bacon-wrapped, cheese-covered, yummy food. It doesn't take long to realize that your low-fat, low-sodium, lots of fresh fruits and veggies diet just isn't going to happen this evening. Then, two thoughts come to mind. First, you think to yourself, *Oh well, today will have to be a cheat day, and if I'm going to cheat, I might as well cheat big and enjoy it.* You determine that what you really want is the triple-decker cheeseburger with french fries and a chocolate shake... Oh, and super-size that, please!

But then you realize there is a second option. Instead of going all out and blowing the diet completely, you could order a hamburger, small side of fries and a diet soft drink. Technically, this would still be a cheat on the diet, but it would allow you to not stray too far off-track. Suddenly, you're startled out of your menu pondering by a voice asking to take your order. The pressure is on... What will you do?

Let's step back for a minute to analyze both of these possibilities more closely. If you decide on the first option, it's obvious that you made a bad choice. You not only ate food that was outside the parameters of your diet, you also consumed a whole lot of it.

Interestingly enough, if you chose the second option you will have also made a bad choice because all of the items in the second list are outside of the guidelines of your healthy-eating plan as well. Neither option is a particularly good choice as far as your diet is concerned; however, the second option is the best bad choice, meaning that you would have done the best you could with what you had to work with.

MAKE THE BEST BAD CHOICE

Making the best bad choice involves moving beyond black-and-white thinking and learning how to pick the most desirable shade of grey. If your life was like mine, childhood was much simpler than life as an adult. In childhood cartoons, the distinction between good guys and bad guys was clear. Heroes were brave, compassionate champions, who would continue to do right regardless of the cost. Villains, on the other hand, were greedy, haters of anything beautiful. They were mean to puppies and children, and endlessly strove to bring their plans for world domination into fruition.

In childhood cartoons, every character had a specific role to play and rarely strayed from their assigned part. Similarly, in Sunday school, black-and-white thinking would be further reinforced as the teacher outlined certain actions that were always good and others that were all bad. The line was clear with little grey in between. While this is not by any means a bad way for children to learn, there eventually comes a point where a shift to a much deeper way of thinking must take place.

A black-and-white perspective of the world keeps things simple, but it is also simplistic and one sign of immaturity. In the real world there is right, there is wrong and there are many situations where we are able to form an ideal picture of what we would like to have happen in our heads, but achieving that ideal is out of reach. Like the fast-food illustration previously mentioned, there will be circumstances where there appears to be no "good option" available. When this happens, it's time to make the best bad choice.

If you find yourself stuck in a situation where there are no easy answers and you realize that you must decide between a multitude of less-than-ideal selections, here are some strategies to help you make the best bad choice.

Strategies for Making the Best Bad Choice

1. Acknowledge that the choice is not what you would have preferred and then move forward in gaining positive momentum.

Discovering that an ideal choice isn't readily available is frustrating. It can throw us off-balance and, in cases where a person decides to wait for better options, can result in becoming stuck, because in some cases, the ideal may not be obtainable. Fortunately, in many instances, what we perceive to be a bad choice is more about perspective than a decision that is truly good or bad.

For example, college students who bemoan the fact that they did not get accepted into the school of their dreams and now must choose between a plethora of "bad" schools may feel like they are making an appalling decision. But is going to college really a bad choice? Of course not! It might feel bad to choose a college that our heart is not set on, but this is hardly a negative decision. Similarly, those starting out in a new career sometimes feel that they must choose between a variety of bad starting jobs. But is there really such a thing as a bad job? When it comes to working and earning money, having something is almost always better than remaining unemployed. And the sooner a person makes the decision to join the work-force, the sooner that person will strengthen their resume, gain valuable experience and build the positive references need to transition to a more desirable position.

Even in the scenario at the beginning of this chapter, stopping at the restaurant was not truly a bad choice but a less desirable one. Breaking for food is better than continuing the journey hungry, tired and grumpy. Having to decide between a number of imperfect options is a normal part of life. But if you lean toward perfectionism, this can be especially difficult to do. Acknowledging that the option we are choosing is less than ideal, grieving the loss and then moving forward can make letting go of our perfectionist tendencies easier and allows us to take the first step toward regaining positive momentum.

2. Use the sound mind that God has given you.

2 Timothy 1:7 says, God has "not given us a spirit of fear, but of power and of love and of a sound mind." God's desire is that you and I be sound-minded, and making the best bad decision involves putting the sound mind that God has given us to work.

One simple strategy for putting clear-headed thinking into practice is to make a pros and cons list. This is accomplished by folding a piece of paper in half, writing the positives of the decision on one side of the paper and the negatives on the other. This simple technique is one of the most powerful tools I know for deciding between two difficult options.

When creating this list, it's important to brainstorm as many pros and cons as you can think of and to write them all down, even when they seem insignificant. There is something about the process of having all of the information laid out in front of you that helps brings clarity to difficult situations. If you want to go the extra mile, you can combine this tool with the next step by enlisting the help of others in forming your list.

3. Seek wise counsel.

God designed us to function best within the context of community. In the book of Genesis, God stated that it was not good for man to be alone. The third strategy for making the best choice when deciding between two undesirable options is to put God's plan for cooperation with others into practice by seeking wise counsel. The Bible is filled with exhortations to seek wise advice from others. For example:

- Proverbs 12:15 says, "The one who listens to advice is wise."
- Proverbs 11:14 states, "There is success in the abundance of counselors."
- And James 1:5 encourages believers to turn to God when they are in need of wisdom, stating, "But if anyone is deficient in wisdom, he should ask God, who gives to all generously

and without reprimand, and it will be given to him."

Not only has God granted us with a sound mind to use when faced with difficult decisions, He has also provided us with other human beings for support, and promises to provide us with wisdom when we ask.

At times life is hard, and being faced with difficult decisions is a normal part of the journey. Learning to make the best bad choice is a powerful strategy for not getting bogged down in the decision-making process. It frees us up to let go of the ideal pictures we build up in our head and encourages us to do the best we can with the options available. Making the best bad choice is about learning to accept reality as it is and move forward with life. So next time you are faced with two frustrating options and don't know what to do next, instead of staying stuck where you are, remember to reach into your toolbox and make the best bad choice.

Chapter 4

Focus on the Good

Marriage and family therapists are well known for asking a lot of questions, and like most therapists, I have plenty of questions in my repertoire. However, in my mind there is one inquiry that stands apart from all others in its ability to elevate a person's attitude and stir up positive momentum in the problem solving process. Don't worry, it's not the famous, "How does that make you feel?" question that therapists are renowned for asking.

Instead, my favorite inquiry is this: "What is going well?" Since the majority of people come to therapy to talk about their problems, asking this tends to throw people off balance, and it's fun watching the confused looks on people's faces. But these looks are also very telling. When faced with problems, our natural tendency is to dwell on the difficulties while paying less attention to the positives in our lives. This is unfortunate because the more we focus on our problems, the more power we give to them. If we're not careful, these challenges will become magnified in our minds, making them even more difficult to manage.

On the other hand, when we focus on things that are going well, the opposite occurs. Attending to the positives magnifies the good in our lives, generating creative energy and momentum that propels us forward in the problem-solving process. I love asking this question because it is a way of taking a strength-based approach to overcoming difficulties. As we will see, this rock-star question has many practical applications for leaders and relaters.

Focus on the Good

Finding the Good

Have you ever experienced a time when problems felt overwhelming? I have. It is a painful, disorienting and helpless feeling. Unfortunately, when we are down and depressed, good solutions rarely feel good at the time because of the negative state of mind we are in. This can hinder us from taking action and cause us to remain stuck where we are.

When providing support to those feeling overwhelmed, you might notice that their troubles don't appear unmanageable, yet from their perspective these challenges appear enormous. Feeling down and depressed has a way of magnifying problems and the same thing can happen to us if we're not careful. When crisis hits and our difficulties becomes the primary area of focus, it causes us to quickly lose momentum, creativity, and motivation. Soon the challenges appear bigger than they actually are, and a negative, self-defeating attitude sets in, resulting in the problems become even more difficult to resolve.

The good news is that the slow, energy draining squeeze of a negative mindset can be adverted by taking the time to acknowledge the good in our lives. Whether you are a leader providing support to someone who has lost momentum, or are in need of a boost to pull yourself out of a slump, focusing on the positives can help. Here are three simple strategies for finding the good.

1. Start small.

No matter how dreary the circumstances appear, there is always—yes always— something good happening, the trick is to find it. If you notice the answers to the question "What's going well?" are not flowing easily, the best thing to do is to start small. It's normal for the discovery of the first few positives to be the most taxing, but don't give up. Generating momentum is the key to building more momentum. I've watched time and time again as those struggling with this question began by giving simple answers. Then, as the energy built, they were able to identify a few additional positives, leading to the discovery of even more after that. It's fun to watch faces light-up as those who engage in this exercise examine their list, come to the realization of just how many things are going right with their life and regain a sense of hope.

If you continue to have difficulty thinking of things that are going well, here are a few ideas to get you started. As you glance through the list, read out loud the ones that apply to you.

- I'm alive and breathing.
- The sun is shining.
- I have a home to live in.
- I have family who loves me.

- I have at least one friend who cares about me.
- I got to enjoy a good cup of coffee, tea, or other favorite beverage today.
- I know that God loves me.
- I have a job.
- In spite of all that I've been through I'm still smiling.
- My parents and children love me.
- My dog (or other pet) is happy to see me when I come home.
- I have time to relax and read this book.

While you may not have everything on this list going for you, I'm willing to bet that at least a few of these apply. Now that you have momentum in your favor, I would encourage you to build on it by writing down three more answers to the question "What's going well?"

1._____
2._____
3._____

Could you do it? If not, you might want to ask a friend or family member to help. During times when we are really hurting, it's important to have close friends to support us in bearing our burdens. Oh, and don't feel bad about asking others for assistance. Galatians 6:2 says, "Carry one another's burdens, and in this way you will fulfill the law of Christ."

When you reach out in your time of need, you're not being a burden, but are providing others with the opportunity to support a friend and fulfill a biblical command. It's good for you and great for your friends. So the next time you find yourself hurting, be sure not to deprive others of the opportunity to serve and support.

2. Play the "if... then..." game.

The "if... then... game" is a fun twist to finding the good. It was 2 a.m. and I was working the overnight shift at a local home for troubled teens. Everyone was asleep and I was feeling down. The hours between 2 a.m. and 5 a.m. were always the most taxing. I had just taken out the trash and was about to sit down and feel sorry for myself. On this particular night I was starting to believe that I couldn't do anything right.

Although the next part of the story is somewhat personal and a little silly, I'm going to share it anyway because it demonstrates the power of finding the good by using the "if... then..." game. Before sitting down to mope, I thought to myself... *I did just take out the trash and I did it well. If I can take out the trash well, **then** I bet I can clean the stove well too.* Next thing I knew I was standing before the stove, cleaning rag in hand. As I began my attack on the previous day's food splatterings, I thought, *I'm doing a* *good job at this overnight position and I bet that **if** I can do a good job at this position, **then** I'll do a really good job when I finish school and start my new career as a therapist too.*

But then another thought hit... *What if I never finish?* Yep, it's easy to think negative thoughts when it's 2 a.m. and you're the only one awake. So I began disputing this idea in my head, thinking to myself... *I did really well in the classes I took so far and **if** I did all right in those classes **then** I have the ability to do just fine in the next classes I take too.* These "if... then..." thoughts kept me moving throughout the remainder of the night. The next thing I knew, it was 5 a.m. I was working hard, feeling much better and most certainly not wallowing in self-pity.

As you can see, this game is simple. It involves looking to past successes to build momentum and predict positive outcomes in the future. This particular tool is especially applicable for who are in school. For example, students who are overwhelmed by a term paper might state to themselves, *I just wrote a sentence and **if** I can write one sentence **then** I can write another. And **if** I can write another sentence, **then** I can write another and another, until I have an entire paragraph. And **if** I can write a paragraph, **then** I can write two, then three, then four. **If** I have the ability to write that many paragraphs, **then** I am fully capable of completing this assignment.*

Don't underestimate the power of breaking seemingly overwhelming tasks into small, achievable objectives and then cheering yourself on each time you take a tiny step forward in the process.

The if... then... Game

In the college classes I teach, most students do exceedingly well. However, each year, a handful do not, and the primary reason for this is a failure to complete the course assignments. Having been a student myself, I understand how difficult it can be to get started. Using the "if... then..." technique is one strategy students can use to build momentum and keep themselves motivated. I am convinced that if more students used this simple technique they would discover they are fully capable of finishing assignments they initially viewed as beyond their capabilities.

3. Look to God for strength.

Feeling down at times is a normal part of life. Our bodies follow predictable patterns of rising and falling. After experiencing an elevation in mood, a de-escalation in energy is a normal next-step that allows our bodies time to recharge. Unfortunately, Christians can take these down times especially hard. This comes from embracing the faulty thinking that life with Christ must be happy and wonderful all of the time. But this belief just doesn't align with reality or Scripture. Sometimes life is hard, and life with Jesus can be tough too.

Trials and periods of unhappiness don't signify a lack of faith. We know this because Jesus told His disciples in John 16:33 that in this world they would have trouble. In addition, David, the renowned giant-slayer, biblical author and king, was also well acquainted with trouble and grief. Yet this didn't prevent him from being recognized as a man after God's own heart, and fortunately, when challenges hit, David had an effective strategy for managing them. David looked for the good by praising God for His greatness.

1 Samuel 30:6 provides the account of a time when David was down. The men who once followed his leadership were now plotting his death. Not only would this have been terrifying, but I imagine David must have felt an enormous weight of betrayal as those closest to him conspired against him. In light of these circumstances, David could have chosen to wallow in self-pity. The situation certainly warranted it. But David was a leader who took charge, brought himself back to a healthy state of mind and began leading well once again.

So how did David regain his positive outlook? 1 Samuel 3:6 says, "But David drew strength from the LORD his God." During difficulties, David looked to God for strength and you and I would be wise to do the same. Many of the Psalms in Scriptures, including those composed by David, begin sorrowfully and end with rejoicing. These passages start with the focus on the insurmountability of the problem. Then, a gradual shift to God's goodness takes place, which leads to increased confidence and finally to jubilation. When our eyes are fixated on God's greatness, might and willingness to intervene in our lives, problems appear much less threatening.

Here are some tools from Scripture for focusing on God's goodness. You may want to read these passages out loud, memorize them and recite them during difficult moments as a means of getting your eyes off of the problem and focusing on His strength.

- Romans 8:28 says, "We know that all things work together for good for those who love God, who are called according to his purpose."

God is willing and able to take the challenges we face and work them for our good and His glory.

- Psalm 118:6, "The LORD is on my side, I am not afraid! What can people do to me?"

The obvious answer to this rhetorical question is "nothing," or at least nothing of any lasting significance. With God on your side, no one and nothing can hinder God's will from being accomplished in you and through you.

- Romans 8:38-39, "For I am convinced that neither death, nor life... nor things that are present, nor things to come... nor anything else in creation will be able to separate us from the love of God in Christ Jesus our Lord."

In spite of the past and regardless of the present, God loves you exactly as you are — and that is something very good.

When problems arise, it can be all too easy to get bogged down with worry and anxiety. Fortunately this doesn't have to be the case. It's possible to regain momentum and use that drive to push through the challenges we face, and it all begins with focusing on the good!

Chapter 5

Reframe the Problem

It was a golden opportunity for revenge and retribution was unmistakably warranted. Joseph was only a boy when his older brothers discarded him. First, they tossed him into an empty well. The prior scuffle that ensued was brief. Ten older brothers against one younger were hardly fair odds. At first, Joseph viewed his brothers' actions as a bad-natured practical joke—one more instance of brothers' picking on brothers in sometimes cruel and thoughtless ways.

As Joseph sat at the bottom of the pit waiting, he thought to himself, *Just give it some time, and this too will pass.* He fully expected his brothers to pull him up at any moment and make amends—and Joseph would have been right, if only Reuben hadn't selected such an inopportune time to depart on his errand. As the eldest brother, Reuben was the leader of the bunch. He was benevolent, but also timid which only added to Joseph's troubles. Although Reuben had no desire to see Joseph get hurt, he was too weak to take a stand. Not wanting to rock the boat, Reuben figured he would let his brothers have their fun and haul

Joseph out of the well after tensions subsided. Unfortunately for Joseph, while Reuben was away, the brothers sold him to a passing group of slave traders—an abrupt and ill-fated turn of events.

Years passed and Joseph's life had many ups and downs. Initially he served as a slave in the home of a kind man by the name of Potiphar. Then, accused of a crime he didn't commit, Joseph was imprisoned. Joseph's trustworthy character earned him a position of prominence in the penitentiary and although being awarded the title of head prisoner wasn't much, Joseph was grateful for it. Then, in a divine twist, Pharaoh, the ruler of all Egypt, had a dream which Joseph interpreted. As a result, Joseph was instantly elevated from prisoner to second in command of all of Egypt.

Years passed. Joseph married and ruled wisely. Then, a great famine hit the land and due to Joseph's prudent leadership, Egypt was one of the few places prepared with sufficient food. Life was good, but then things got even better. One day, Joseph watched in amazement as his brothers entered his presence requesting to buy food. The brothers didn't recognize Joseph and a series of tests took place before he exposed his true identity. When Joseph finally revealed himself as the brother sold into slavery, his siblings were terrified. Each one wondered how Joseph would exact his well deserved revenge. This truly was the ideal occasion for Joseph to pay his brothers back for the time he spent as a prisoner and a slave.

But instead of vengeance, Joseph offered forgiveness. Bitterness, rage and anger had no power over him and Joseph made it clear to his brothers why this had happened, stating, "As for you, you meant to harm me, but God intended it for a good purpose, so he could preserve the lives of many people, as you can see this day"(Genesis 5:20). Instead of becoming bitter, Joseph used the challenges he faced as an opportunity to become better and he did this by reframing his circumstances. In Joseph's mind, the events that happened to him were not horrible, awful and evil. Instead, they were an opportunity for God to work mightily in his life to save many people from the horrors of starvation.

Reframing Our Circumstances

Like Joseph, we too can erase feelings of anger, bitterness and frustration, replacing them with peace, contentment and joy by reframing our circumstances. Reframing involves altering our perspective. Like a painting that is taken out of an old, tattered picture-frame and placed in a new one, the tool of reframing involves removing a negative view of our situation and making the intentional choice to view these same events in a more positive light. In reframing, things that were once perceived as horrible, awful and terrible transform into opportunities, adventures and good stories.

Framing and Reframing

Which frame will you choose?

Overcoming Objections to Reframing

One objection to reframing is that it is nothing more than overly optimistic, pie-in-the-sky thinking that doesn't really help anyone — and when used incorrectly, this can be the case. However, for our purposes, reframing will not be an exercise in pretending that a negative event is actually a positive one. Trying to do this is just plain silly and certainly doesn't help anyone.

Reframing works because it causes us to evaluate the reality and validity of our thoughts. The goal of reframing is twofold. First, it is to eliminate our natural tendency toward stinking thinking and second, when there are two reasonable ways of viewing our situation, the goal is to choose the more positive of the two rational and realistic options.

Eliminating Stinking Thinking

The well-known psychologist and founder of rational emotive behavioral therapy, Albert Ellis, spoke of people's natural tendency to upset themselves by awfulizing their situation. To awfulize something is to magnify the negative aspects of the event. Ellis used the word "awfulize" because he believed that very few events in life could truly be categorized as "awful." Sad yes, disappointing, frustrating, and a nuisance, absolutely! But in most cases, describing an event as awful just doesn't line up with reality.

Choosing the Positive

What if life events were not really good or bad so much as they were neutral events that we added our opinion to? A famous line from William Shakespeare's *Hamlet* says, "For there is nothing either good or bad, but thinking makes it so." This short phrase is packed with meaning. In most instances, it's how we choose to view the event that makes all of the difference.

Joseph's life is a brilliant illustration of Shakespeare's point. Was being sold into slavery a bad thing for Joseph? I for one, am not so sure that it was. While it was most certainly unpleasant, if it hadn't happened, Joseph never would have been elevated to a position of leadership in Egypt. Now, let's look at a second example. What about getting fired from a job? Is this bad? Some would treat it that way and use it as an excuse to bemoan and complain about how unfair the world is. Others would take full advantage of the opportunity by reevaluating their profession, developing new skills and discovering a vocation that is more aligned with their passions. Are you starting to get the idea? What initially appears "bad" may not be as horrific as it first seems, and in some cases it may end up being a blessing in disguise.

Opportunities, Adventures and Good Stories

How we feel about what happens to us is directly related to the stories we tell ourselves about the events happening around us. These stories are often told silently in our heads. Therapists refer to them as self-talk and it is something that everyone does. Negative self-talk brings us down, while positive reframes are types of energizing self-talk that help us to get back on track.

Opportunities, adventures and good stories are three of my favorite reframes that are used to focus on the positive side of life's obstacles. For example:

- Failing a test could be reframed an opportunity to learn better study habits.

- Getting lost while driving could be reframed as an adventure.

- Odd twists and turns in life, such as getting mistaken for the computer repair man at work, can be reframed as a good story to tell later... and it's all right: I've fully embraced the fact that I look more like an electrician, computer repair man and "the internet guy" than a marriage and family therapist. These mistakes happen all the time and really do make for a fun story.

Next time you're facing a challenge, see if you can reframe the problem in a more positive light by asking the following questions:

- Does this challenge offer the opportunity to learn, grow or make improvements to any area of my life?
- Is there something exciting about what is happening that would allow me to reframe these circumstances as an adventure?
- Could this be a good story to tell and something that I can laugh about later? If so, can I laugh about it now?

This last question might help you to keep your sense of humor in-tact in the midst of trying times. This is important because a little humor goes a long way in not only changing our attitude, but also the entire feel of a situation. Reframing is a vital skill for leaders and relaters because it helps to keep our attitude in check. When the leader's attitude is hopeful and upbeat, others will follow suit. So next time you find yourself facing a challenging situation, remember to avoid the trap of stinking thinking by finding the opportunity, adventure and good story to tell and in so doing, reframe the problem.

Chapter 6

Take Care of You

It was just before dawn and everyone else in the house was asleep. The man rose silently, pulled on his robe and softly made his way outside. There was no time for sleeping in. What was about to happen was far too important. With only the moon and stars for light, the man cautiously made his way through the windy streets to a dirt path on the outskirts of town. As he walked, the man thought about the many pressing needs of the day. There were sick people in need of healing, teaching to be done and dear friends to attend to ... but for now, all of that could wait.

By the time he reached the edge of town, the stars had faded and the sun had begun its ascent. The man increased his pace; following the narrow dirt path up a slight incline. There was no time to waste. Soon the world would be awake and the day would officially begin—and what a whirlwind of a day it would be. Just like the day before, and the day before that. Once the hustle and bustle began, the pace never slowed.

Finally, the man reached his destination. Out of breath and eager to begin, he found a mid-sized rock perfect for sitting that provided a spectacular view of the valley below. Then this man did what he came to do. He sat down, took a few deep breaths, watched, listened and began to pray. While he sat, the stress of the previous days melted away, and as he prayed, the pressures of the weeks ahead diminished. He and His Heavenly Father were in this together. Yes, there was much to accomplish, and in spite of the effort put forth, there would still be and abundance of work to be done. But for now, none of that mattered. What was imperative was that Jesus found strength for the day.

By this time, the sun had fully risen. Jesus' friends were awake and two of them had managed to find Him. Now, it was time for the day to officially begin, and Jesus was ready for it. He had accomplished what he had set out to do. He had spent time with His Father, He had stepped away from the pressures of the work needing to be done, sat, rested, cleared His head and soaked in a few moments of wonderful silence. Refreshed and renewed, Jesus descended the hill with his companions, ready to embark on the next leg of the adventure.

Although I'm not sure if the event happened in precisely this manner, we do know that it happened. Mark 1:35 says, "Then Jesus got up early in the morning when it was still very dark, departed, and

76

went out to a deserted place, and there he spent time in prayer." Jesus took time to pause and step away from his work in order to take care of himself. If Jesus needed time for self-care, it is only reasonable to expect that you and I do as well.

But finding time to recharge can be complicated, and it certainly isn't getting any easier. This story didn't happen by accident. Jesus had to intentionally make time to step away, and this was before the days of cell phones, e-mail and computers. Today there is more to do than ever before, which is why getting into the habit of good self-care is so important. To better understand the importance of self-care, consider the following:

You are Responsible for Taking Care of You

Sometime people avoid self-care, viewing it as selfish, while in reality it's just the opposite. Attending to our own needs puts us in a healthy place that allows us to reach out to others from a place of abundance. We cannot impart to others something we do not possess ourselves, and if we try to care for others from a place of emptiness, there is a good chance that we will end up doing more harm than good. It's almost impossible to maintain a positive attitude when we are overly tired, stressed out, and emotionally drained, and the increased irritability these things bring makes it especially easy to hurt those closest to us.

The busier life gets, the more important good self-care becomes.

Practicing good self-care is particularly important for those who are married. Husbands and wives, your spouse needs you to take care of you because while your spouse can do a lot of things for you, he or she does not possess the ability to make you happy. You have the ultimate responsibility when it comes to managing your own emotions and being a content spouse really is a gift to your partner because it provides them with a sense of peace and stability.

For example, wives, your husband has the ability to cook for himself, even if it's limited to defrosting a frozen pizza. Men are natural hunters, gatherers and survivors. If a nice, home-cooked meal isn't waiting for your husband when he walks in the door, he will find a way to get by—I promise. However, men don't have the ability to make their wives happy, and the same is true for wives. Each person's level of contentment is something that they must take charge of. When we take responsibility for managing our emotions through good self-care, it provides our spouses with the freedom to breathe easy and relax.

But don't just take my word for it, Proverbs 15:17 says, "Better a meal of vegetables where there is love than a fattened ox where there is hatred." And Proverbs 21:19 says, "It is better to live in a desert land than with a quarrelsome and easily-provoked woman." Without gas a car won't run and if you and I don't make time to fill up our self-care tanks we won't function very well either. Taking time to recharge is a must if we are going to lead and connect well. Here are three strategies for putting healthy self-care into practice.

Simple Strategies for Good Self-Care:

1. Make self-care a priority.

Jesus modeled self-care and you, and I would be wise to follow His example. If you find yourself exceedingly busy, then you may need to make self-care the first activity of the day. If you have a larger family like I do, early mornings may be the only time that you have to yourself. Here are a few other strategies for becoming intentional in the practice of good self-care.

- Schedule it.

Setting aside time for yourself can be done by setting an alarm to help you wake up earlier or by intentionally blocking off a set amount of time on the calendar specifically for you, to take care of you.

- Plan ahead.

If you are anything like me there are days where you feel like you're living in a time warp. You plan to relax but end up getting caught up in activity instead. The next thing you know, you find yourself looking up at the clock wondering, *What just happened, where did all of the time go?* I've found that it's all too easy to intellectually understand the importance of good self-care, but end up checking e-mail, running that quick errand, getting caught up in a television show and cleaning up yesterday's messes instead. Don't let this happen to you. Instead, take charge by deciding exactly how you will spend your self-care time before it begins. Will you read a book, journal, pray, go for a walk, take a bubble bath or listen to your favorite music? By planning out specific care activities we can avoid falling into the time warp-trap.

- Enlist the help of others

As a father of three, it would be nearly impossible to find the time to take a break without the support of my wife. Ecclesiastes 4:9 says, "Two people are better than one, because they can reap more benefit from their labor." And the more people that you add to your team, the better. You and I were not made to go through life alone and if you have children, a tag-team approach to self-care is a must.

2. Unplug.

Making time for healthy self-care isn't easy and it's not getting any easier. With computers, cell phones and video streaming, there is more to do and see than ever before. Work, friends and non-stop entertainment are easily accessed from the comfort of home. Not that plugging in is all bad; it's just not a substitute for healthy aerobic exercise, prayer, and real face-to-face connections.

Failing to un-plug is a trap that I have to be especially mindful about not to falling into. I love getting up early to read and write. I've noticed my tendency to check e-mail first thing in the morning just to make sure that nothing urgent is waiting, but I've come to learn that as soon as I open my in-box, the time for self-care is officially over. There are never any lack of distractions clamoring for my attention once I am inside, and the only way to stay on track is to avoid the temptation of taking that first look until I'm ready for the day to begin. The second strategy for practicing good self-care goes along with the first. Not only do we need to be intentional about making time for self-care, we also need to be purposeful in guarding these precious moments against time-consuming, non-recharging activities.

3. Use the right fuel.

A few years ago, I embarked on a rescue mission to help a stranded family member who had mistakenly filled the gas tank of her car with diesel fuel. It wasn't long before thick black smoke came pouring over the hood. With the help of a tow truck, we transported the car to a nearby auto repair shop. Fortunately, no real damage was done.

Like a car, you and I need the right fuel to function at our best. There are a variety of different ways to practice healthy self-care. Taking time away from the hustle and bustle of life is crucial, and of equal importance is practicing healthy self-care activities throughout the day. As previously mentioned, we are biopsychosocial beings — our body, mind and spirit are intertwined. On days that we are hungry, overly tired, sick or stressed out, not only is our physical body impacted, but our thoughts and relationships are as well. Consistent care is needed in order for us to function well, so it's imperative that self-care be an ongoing process as opposed to a one-time event. Taking care of ourselves throughout the day can involve the following:

- Making healthy food choices

Too much sugar, salt, alcohol, caffeine and fatty foods are a surefire way to feel down and sluggish. Stress eating, something that I can be guilty of myself at times, is similar to filling a car with diesel fuel: the tank gets filled, but the car doesn't run well. During times of high stress, going out of the way to maintain a healthy diet is a simple but powerful strategy for maintaining good self-care.

• Exercising regularly

Studies have shown that regular aerobic exercise, such as walking, jogging and swimming, are equally as powerful in warding off depression as medication and therapy. Becoming intentional about engaging in healthy physical activity on a routine basis has the ability to alter our entire outlook on life.

• Getting sufficient sleep

Sleep deficiency reduces reaction time, decreases memory, promotes poor performance and diminishes one's mood. If you've ever been sleep-deprived, then took the time to catch up on the rest you've been missing, then you know that a good night's rest can improve one's entire perspective on life.

According to Psalm 139:14, you are fearfully and wonderfully made. There is no one else like you and no one else who can fulfill your unique role on earth. Yet the only person who can keep you healthy is you. In order to lead and connect to others well, it is vital that we operate from a place of abundance. When the storms of life hit, good leaders take care of themselves, which allows them to move through the trying times gracefully and emerge on the other side stronger and wiser than before.

By taking time to fill our own tanks, we are then able to reach out to others from a place of healthy abundance. The world needs this kind of leader, but the only way for this to happen is for you to take good care of you.

Chapter 7

From Surviving to Thriving

God's will is that you and I not only survive, but thrive. In John 10:10, Jesus said that He came so that we could have life and have it abundantly. But what exactly does having an abundant life look like? If we asked twenty different people, it is likely that we would get twenty different answers. Happiness is elusive and there are no shortage of opinions when it comes to ideas of what life is all about. Some would say that living abundantly means:

- Earning a lot of money
- Feeling good about oneself
- Relaxing and living a life of ease
- Maintaining one's physical health
- Living a life that is conflict free, or
- Having a whole lot of fun

While all of these things are good, none of them describes what it truly means to thrive. The life that God calls us to may or may not entail the items listed above. When it comes to living an abundant life, there are two errors that Christ's followers often make and both are on opposite ends of the spectrum. The first mistake is to believe that Christ calls us to a life of rest, relation and ease. Late-night television is consumed with prosperity preachers touting that all Christians should be healthy, wealthy and wise. Sickness is viewed as sign of a lack of faith and physical and financial prosperity are heralded as readily available to all who will receive them. In the minds of some, the normal Christian life is smooth, calm and conflict-free.

While this sounds nice, it is much different from what Jesus taught. In John 16:33, Jesus told His disciples, "In the world you (will) have trouble and suffering." Pain and conflict are a normal part of life. They are characteristic of living in a fallen world. While it's true that some Christians prosper financially, others do not. Similarly, some are fit and strong while others wrestle with physical and mental illnesses all their lives. Neither is an indicator of faith nor a lack of it.

The world we live in is one of beauty and conflict. It is a good world, created by a loving God that is also under a curse of sin and death. Both pain and pleasure are a normal part of life. According to Matthew 5:45, God "causes the sun to rise on the evil and the good, and sends rain on the righteous and the unrighteous." Neither prosperity nor anguish are guaranteed.

This brings us to the other end of the spectrum. On one hand, God does not promise a life of ease; on the other hand, He does not encourage us to pursue pain. Just as some teach that prosperity is a sign of faith, others believe that the God-honoring life must consist of suffering, and sorrow. In ages past, men and women isolated themselves in monasteries, refused to marry, dined meagerly and abstained from earthy pleasures. Some went so far as to intentionally inflict pain upon their own bodies, because they equated suffering as a sign of spirituality.

Yet this type of life is not something the Bible compels us to peruse either. Psalm 84:11 says, "For the LORD God is our sovereign protector. The LORD bestows favor and honor; he withholds no good thing from those who have integrity." But how do we reconcile this Scripture with Jesus' teaching? One passage promises that while on earth, suffering will be a part of our journey, while the other proclaims that God will not withhold any good thing from those who trust in Him.

As we will see from the life of the Apostle Paul, the normal Christian life is a paradox. These two scriptures are neither contradictory nor irreconcilable, but complement each other well. In 2 Corinthians 6:5-10, the Apostle Paul demonstrates how both distress and delight is possible in the same moment when he writes,

*"But as God's servants, we have commended ourselves in every way, with great endurance, in persecutions, in difficulties, in distresses, in beatings, in imprisonments, in riots, in troubles, in sleepless nights, in hunger... through glory and dishonor, through slander and praise; regarded as impostors, and yet true; as unknown, and yet well-known; **as dying and yet – see!** – we continue to live; as those who are scourged and yet not executed; **as sorrowful, but always rejoicing,** as poor, but making many rich, **as having nothing, and yet possessing everything."***

This is precisely what it means to live the abundant life that Christ calls us to. A life of ease is not promised, nor is a life of suffering commanded. Neither wealth nor poverty, sickness nor health, happiness nor sorrow is a true test of faith. Sunny days and stormy nights come upon the just and unjust alike. Yet for the Christ follower there is peace in the midst of pain and joy in spite of sorrows. Even if one day we were to find ourselves with no earthly possessions, we would know that although we have nothing, in Christ we possess everything!

In this book, we examined five tools for building leadership, growing relationships and increasing overall wellbeing. The goal of learning these skills is not to make life trouble-free. Problems will continue to exist until that great and glorious day when Christ returns. Then and only then will Eden lost become Eden restored. Until then, you and I live in a world of tension, where both beauty and chaos exist side by side—a good world, created by a loving God, under the curse of sin and death.

The lessons in this book are about learning to manage these complex tensions well. At times life is hard, while at other times it is filled with beauty, wonder and awe. The goal of applying these five simple strategies is to make sure that life's challenges are not any more difficult than they need to be. When the storms of life hit, it is possible to move through these trying times with dignity and grace. But this is not the only goal. Life is so much more than our trials; there are also many wonderful times, and these tools help us to make the most out of the joyful moments in life. But it doesn't stop there, using these tools leads us to a place of abundance that allows us to come alongside of those who are hurting and guide them down a path of healing—a journey that we are well acquainted with because we first traveled it ourselves.

The next time you find yourself face-to-face with a leadership obstacle or relational challenge I invite you to put the principles of letting go of the rope, making the best bad choice, finding the good, reframing the problem and taking care of you into practice and witness the dynamic results these powerful tools bring. The more frequently you implement these strategies, the easier and more natural they will become.

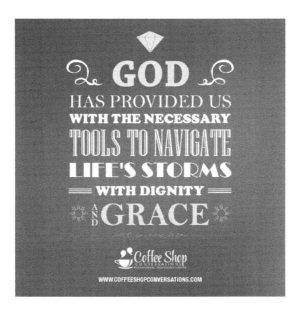

2 Peter 3:18 says, "But grow in the grace and knowledge of our Lord and Savior Jesus Christ." I am thrilled that you chose to make this book a part of your growth journey and wish you the best as you continue to honor God and further develop your skills in the areas of leadership and relationships.

Tools for Living Well

Don't Pick UP the Rope
1 Offer choices.
2 Give empathy.
3 Accentuate areas of agreement.
4 Allow teachable moments to take place.

Make the best bad choice
1 Acknowledge the choice is not ideal, then gain back momentum.
2 Use the sound mind God has given you.
3 Seek wise counsel.

Focus on the good
1 Start small.
2 Play the "if... then..." game.
3 Look to God for strength.

Reframe the Problem
1 Focus on the opportunity.
2 Make it an adventure.
3 Find the good story to tell.

Take care of you
1 Make self-care a priority.
2 Unplug.
3 Use the right fuel.

Glimpses of God

Taken from *Coffee Shop Conversations: Psychology and the Bible; Building Leaders, Growing Relationships.*

Henry Ward Beecher, a pastor, speaker, and social reformist, well known in the eighteen hundreds, once stated, "Every artist dips his brush in his own soul, and paints his own nature into his pictures." With artistic brilliance, God fashioned His masterpiece of creation, and these words are just as applicable to Him. If you have ever paused to gaze upon this handiwork, then you are well aware that our universe reflects His splendor.

My most vivid experience of becoming fixated upon God's artistic work of genius occurred during my second year of college. After spending the summer working as a camp counselor, four of the other staff and I piled into a six-passenger minivan and embarked on an adventure to Yosemite National Park. During the eight-hour journey from San Diego to Glacier Point—one of the parks well-known highpoints which has a spectacular view—I was engrossed in conversation and paid little attention to our surroundings.

After hours of non-stop travel, our vehicle finally slowed to a halt. Everyone clambered to get out. It had been a cramped, stuffy drive. Outside, the air was crisp and clean. The trees were a vibrant green, towering and majestic. The scent of pine lingered in the air as the gentle breeze softly rustled through the branches overhead. It was pleasant, far more appealing than the outdoor scenery that I was accustomed to.

We began our trek from the parking lot to the scenic overlook, and as we rounded the bend, Half-Dome, El Capitan, and the valley below came into view. Approaching the overlook, I experienced the burst of excitement that comes with peering down a sheer cliff to a forest 3,000 feet below. Toward the west, Yosemite Falls, the world's fifth tallest waterfall, was rushing in full force. I watched in awe as every second 2,400 gallons of water spilled over the edge of the precipice and plummeted a distance equal to the height of Sears Tower before vanishing into a grove of trees at the bottom. In an instant, this trip had become so much more than pleasant—I was experiencing God's artwork at its finest, and it was breathtaking!

Later that afternoon, the five of us trekked to an open field just below El Capitan, an enormous mass of stone with a steep face that has become a playground for skilled rock climbers from around the world. When evening approached, we stared in admiration as tiny glimmers of light made their appearance on the rock face. Men and women making the multiple-day climb to the top were latching in their sleeping gear and igniting their lanterns in order to do whatever it is rock climbers do before dozing off while suspended hundreds of feet above the earth.

We observed in wonder as the stars emerged on the horizon—first in the form of a few, faint splotches of light; then, within a matter of minutes, the sun fully set, and the sky was enveloped in a flurry of stars that never seemed closer nor shone more brilliantly. As if

on cue, the first shooting star made its appearance —
followed by a second and many more after that.

Ever since this expedition to Yosemite, I have
longed to return. I imagine David having a similar
encounter with the exquisiteness of God's universe
when he wrote:

> *The heavens declare the glory of God; the sky
> displays his handiwork. Day after day it speaks
> out; night after night it reveals his greatness.
> There is no actual speech or word, nor is its voice
> literally heard. Yet its voice echoes throughout
> the earth. (Psalm 19:1-4)*

Something magnificent happens inside of us
when we stumble upon the wonders of God's
creation — His greatness is revealed without a word.
During these times, God's existence isn't questioned;
it is known, because the echo of His voice is clear. Just
as art offers a glance into the into the artist's soul,
nature is God's masterpiece, which provides a
glimpse into the splendor of our Creator.

Upcoming Books

Continue the journey with *Coffee Shop Conversations on the Bible and Psychology; Live, Love and Lead Well*, available November 2014, from Amazon.com.

"An insightful and tender exchange where Biblical truths and psychological principles intersect. Enjoy this refreshing and poignant resource that goes beyond "good advice" while authentically revealing the golden nuggets that can truly penetrate a broken heart."
~ Ramona M. Garretson, *Psy.D., MFT, NCC*

"Jed has a passion for helping people sharpen their leadership and relationship skills at home, work and everywhere they go. *Coffee Shop Conversations,* which reflects Jed's love for God and for people, is a tool to help you make your life count!"
~ Pastor Jim Garlow, *Senior Pastor: Skyline Wesleyan Church*

"Jed's *Coffee Shop Conversations* delivers biblical answers to real-life issues. It will enrich your Christian life—well worth your investment. I encourage you to read it while opening up your life to God's GRACE."
~ Dr. Donald W. Welch, *Ph.D., LMFT, Founder and President, Center for Enriching Relationships*

Continue the Journey

Would you like to take your understanding of theology and psychology to the next level? If so, Southern California Seminary can help. With face-to-face and on-line options, solid Scriptural teachings, and an affordable tuition, Southern California Seminary is an exceptional resource for those longing for high-quality education built upon the solid foundation of God's word!

You can find out more by visiting www.socalsem.edu or by calling (619)-201-8959. We look forward to hearing from you soon.

Continue the Conversation

I hope you enjoyed this book and would love to hear from you. Continue the conversation at:

My blog: www.coffeeshopconversations.com

E-mail: jed@coffeeshopconversations.com

Twitter: @jjurchenko

Facebook: Coffee Shop Conversations

This is my very first book and your feedback is greatly appreciated. I'd also love it if you would post a review on amazon.com. Then, drop me an e-mail letting me know so I can reply and thank you personally.

Made in the USA
San Bernardino, CA
23 December 2014